UNBREAKABLE

IESHA S JENKINS

UNBREAKABLE

CALAMITY MEETS RESILIENCE

Uma's Oasis Corp 929 N Val Vista Dr Suite 109 PMB 1533 Gilbert, AZ 85234 www.umasoasis.com

CONTENTS

CONTENTS

FOREWORD

I have come to a profound realization that in order to truly let go of our pain, we must not only acknowledge it, but also process it with utmost care. It is with great vulnerability and courage that I share my personal journey with you in these pages. Although I had initially hesitated to release this book, as I am still in the midst of processing my own pain, I believe that by sharing my experiences, I can offer a glimmer of hope and healing to others.

This path to healing is still fresh and raw for me, but I can confidently say that I am on the mend. As I embark on this transformative journey, I sincerely hope that something within these words resonates with you and provides solace in some way.

These memories, a tapestry of both joy and pain, have etched themselves deeply into the fabric of my childhood. They have bestowed upon me invaluable lessons about the unyielding power of family, the unwavering spirit required to conquer adversity, and the exquisite beauty found in the most modest of moments. It speaks of yearning, of being forsaken, and of an insatiable hunger for love and acceptance. It is the story of a young girl who longed for love, protection, and stability, grappling with the bewildering question of why she was left behind. It is a narrative of resilience, as I navigate the treacherous waters of pain and seek solace in the embrace of love that I need and owe myself.

Though some of these memories bear the weight of anguish, they have forged me into the person I stand as today. They have illuminated the profound significance of compassion and empathy, as I strive to fathom the struggles of others. They have revealed to me the indomitable strength that resides within the bonds of family, and the unyielding resilience required to endure the hardships that life thrusts upon us. Above all, they have reminded me to treasure the simplest of moments, to find solace and delight amidst the tempestuous storms of adversity.

To my beloved children, Khyturah, Egypt, Naimah, Kairo, and Kian, this book is dedicated to you. You are the very reason I continue to find strength and purpose in life. My love for each of you knows no bounds, and it is with every fiber of my being that I pour my heart into these pages.

May this book serve as a guiding light for those who are seeking solace and healing. May it remind us all that even in our darkest moments, there is always a glimmer of hope waiting to be discovered. Together, let us embark on this journey of healing, knowing that we are never alone.

GOODBYE MOMMY

On one unforgettable morning in September 2006, the world, as I knew it, seemed to halt abruptly. The sharp ring of the telephone tore through the quietude at the ungodly hour of 4:20 am. The pitch darkness outside was a perfect reflection of the heaviness that had settled deep in my heart. The voice that came through the other end was from the hospice nurse. The sorrow that laced her tone was all the confirmation I needed for the fears that had been gnawing at me. My dear mother, the woman who gave me life, had breathed her last.

The news hit me with the force of a tidal wave. It washed over me with such intensity, leaving me numb and breathless. I felt as though I had been thrown into a different dimension, one where the reality of my mother's absence was too hard to grasp.

Despite the raging storm of shock within me, I responded to the nurse in a calm, steady voice, assuring her that I would be on my way to my mother's home.

I gently woke my husband, my voice choked with emotion as I relayed the heartbreaking news. Tears freely flowed down my cheeks, wetting the faces of my two young daughters as I kissed their foreheads tenderly. I bid them farewell, knowing that their worlds would never be the same without the love and guidance of their cherished grandmother. With the weight of the world on my shoulders, I set out on the journey from our home in Bensalem, PA to my mother's house in Roebling, NJ, a house that was once filled with her warmth and love. The drive was a blur as my mind was swallowed by a fog of grief and disbelief.

Pulling into her driveway, the sight of the empty garage hit me with a wave of profound emptiness. It was as though a void had consumed everything, leaving behind an indescribable sense of loss. One by one, my family members began to arrive, their faces full of sorrow, their steps heavy with the weight of their grief. Amidst the pain, I knew I had a responsibility to be there for my grandmother who had just lost her youngest daughter. My mother's words echoed in my mind, pushing me to find the strength within me.

Drawing from the depths of my resilience, I walked into the house, bracing myself for the stark absence of my mother's vibrant spirit. The air was heavy with her absence, the once lively home now felt colorless and desolate. I hugged her weary husband, Jose, who looked both drained and relieved. He had been with her in her final moments, a silent witness to the toll her illness had taken on her. A pang of guilt washed over me for not having stayed over the night before. The hospice nurse had convinced me to rest, but now I found myself questioning that decision. My mother had stopped speaking and eating, her gaze constantly fixed on the corner of the ceiling. Morphine was her only solace, yet her eyes displayed a disconcerting restlessness. I watched as my mother, my sweet mommy, slipped away before my very eyes.

In that moment, I found myself silently begging her to fight, to stay with me. The thought of being left behind was too much to bear. My own desires clouded my judgment, making me blind to her own wishes. Just a week prior, she had shared with me her readiness to depart from this world. She had assured me that I possessed the strength to carry on. Yet, even seventeen years later, I still feel far from okay. Her belief in my resilience has become my guiding light, leading me through the darkest moments of my life.

When my grandmother arrived, the pain on her face was unbearable to witness. I had lost a mother, but she had lost her youngest daughter, a pain unimaginable. The sight of her tears as they placed my mother's lifeless body into the funeral home car shattered my heart into a million pieces. In her grief-stricken state, my grandmother attempted to climb into the vehicle, desperate to be with her daughter one last time. It was then I realized the need to be her pillar of strength, to provide whatever comfort I could in the face of such immense loss.

Carolyn D. Jenkins (Uma)

This chapter of my life, painted in hues of loss and sorrow, continues to resonate within me. The pain remains, a constant reminder of what I lost, a constant ache I carry with me each day. But so does the strength that my mother believed I possessed. Though I am still far from okay, I had to find a resilience within me to carry me forward, even in the face of unimaginable heartache. My mother's passing taught me that life can be cruel and unpredictable, but it also showed me the depths of love and the power of the human spirit. And it is with that knowledge that I continue to navigate this journey called life, forever changed but determined to honor my mother's memory by living a life filled with love, strength, and resilience.

HOW IT STARTED

Growing up, my memories of my dad are hazy, almost non-existent. He was a marine, always away on duty, and I can't even recall if we ever lived together as a family. It wasn't until I was seven years old that I started to form memories with him, but by then, my parents had already separated. I don't remember anyone telling me about their separation, or maybe they did and I just can't recall. It's a blur.

Years later, I discovered the truth. My dad had left and started a new family in North Carolina right after marrying my mom. I remember my mom crying a lot during that time, but eventually, she stopped. She met someone new, my soon-to-be stepdad, and suddenly, she was filled with happiness. She couldn't contain her excitement as she shared the news that I would soon have twin baby brothers. I was overjoyed.

The day I first laid eyes on my twin brothers is engraved in my memory. They were so tiny, so fragile. My mom allowed me to hold "Fat Boy" (Raheem), and it was an incredible feeling to know that he was my baby brother, someone who would live with me. "Skinny Minny" (Hakeem) was too small for me to hold at the time, but he was the most adorable thing I had ever seen. They were perfect in every way, despite their size. And to top it all off, my new dad called me his baby girl. It was a feeling I can't even put into words. Even his older son, Bentley, treated me like his little sister. I finally had a real family.

For a while, everything seemed perfect. I remember going to the mall and riding the merry-go-round with my mom, her smile beaming with joy. But behind her eyes, I could see the pain she was trying to hide. I believed that if I could just be good, if I could make her happy, maybe her sadness would disappear.

As time went on, my new dad started to change. He looked and acted differently. I could sense that something was wrong, but I didn't know how serious it was. Eventually, he became scary to me, and I didn't want to be around him anymore. He spent more and more time in the hospital, and so did my brothers. Then one day, he never came back home. I spent years wondering what had happened to him, where he had gone.

My brothers' health deteriorated over time, and my mom was always busy at the hospital with them. I had to stay with my dad's family, constantly moving from one house to another. Perhaps that's why I find it hard to settle down even now.

During that period, I spent a lot of time at my grandmothers' houses. Luckily, both of them lived across the street from each other, making it easy for me to go back and forth. I stayed with my mom's mom, who I called Grandma, most of the time. She was strict, much stricter than my Grammy, my dad's mom. Whenever

Grandma became too much for me to handle, I would escape to Grammy's house, where I felt a sense of freedom.

Grammy wasn't around as much, but she made up for it with her active lifestyle and mobility. Both grandmothers were deeply spiritual, attending church every Sunday and being involved in various church activities. As a child, I didn't have a choice but to be part of their religious lives. Halloween was considered the devil's holiday, so we were never allowed to celebrate it. Instead, we attended vacation Bible school and choir rehearsals.

Both grandmothers had different households. At Grandma's house, there were strict rules and consequences for breaking them. My cousin Tosha and her brother Al were like siblings to me, and we were often together. We would wake up at 6 am on Saturday mornings to clean the house, scrubbing walls and doing chores. Grammy's house, on the other hand, offered more freedom. We could watch TV, play outside, and enjoy snacks. The best part was being able to sleep in on Saturday mornings. With a multitude of cousins on each side, I had the luxury of choosing who I wanted to spend time with.

When I first discovered that my mom was sick, I was too young to fully comprehend the gravity of the situation. All I knew was that at night, I would hear her cries of agony and see her writhing in pain. The countless trips to the hospital became a regular occurrence, and fear would often grip my heart as I watched her tremble in her sleep, unsure of how to help her. My mom had me when she was just sixteen, and I was her only surviving child. She was my pillar of strength, my hero, and I dreaded the thought of disappointing her. I vividly remember the way people treated her, as if she was somehow lesser, and I yearned to shield her from their cruelty. I longed for more time with her during my younger years, but life had other plans, and she had so much on her plate.

Many nights were spent at my grandmother's house, eagerly awaiting my mom's arrival to pick me up after work. Sometimes, however, she wouldn't show up that night, leaving me in a state of uncertainty. Back then, we didn't have cell phones to communicate easily, so if she called and told me to go to bed, promising to pick me up the next day, I would obediently do so. But if no call came, I would find myself glued to the window, searching for her headlights amidst the darkness, eagerly anticipating her arrival. It didn't matter what time it was, whether it was day or night, I would be overjoyed to see her step out of the car, her heels clicking on the pavement. All I wanted was to go home with my mom, regardless of the hour.

The year was 1985, and amidst the chaos that surrounded me, I struggled to make sense of it all. One moment, I had my mom and my biological father, who were actually married, and then suddenly, they were gone. I remember my mom marrying my new dad, and the arrival of my baby brothers, Hakeem and Ryheem. But people kept disappearing from my life, and my mom was often absent. I recall walking into school one day and feeling like I had entered a different world. No one wanted to talk to me, and I couldn't understand why. As a diligent student, it bewildered me when they called my mom into the office to discuss me. It wasn't until later that I would discover the reason behind the parents' reluctance to let their children play with me. They would stare and point, but no one would extend a hand of friendship.

Eventually, the principal, Miss McGee, summoned my mom to her office, expressing concerns about my continued presence at the school. At that tender age, I couldn't comprehend the gravity of the situation. I had lost my family, and I couldn't fathom why the kids didn't want to be my friends. Prior to all of this, I had a wonderful relationship with the staff at my elementary school. I was a star student, excelling in my studies and even being promoted to the gifted and talented program. I never caused any trouble and always listened to my teachers. So why did they want me out of the school? The rejection and sense of being unwanted weighed heavily on my young heart. I couldn't understand why. I remember staring at a picture of myself at seven years old, wearing a blue and white striped dress. In that moment, I saw a beautiful child, but when I looked in the mirror, I saw ugliness. I convinced myself that it was my own unattractiveness that re-pelled people, and I despised myself. That day, I tore up every picture of myself as a child, desperate to be someone else, any-one else. I yearned to be more interesting, to capture my mom and dad's attention, to make them want to spend time with me. I craved something that would make me worthy of their focus.

I vividly recall a time when I found myself surrounded by people, yet feeling utterly abandoned. Where was my mother? Where was my father? Where were my brothers? Why was I con-stantly staying at other people's houses? The sense of longing and confusion overwhelmed me.

In the midst of all the heartache and loss, I overheard whispers and gossip about my mother from family and friends. I couldn't fully comprehend their words, but I knew they were speaking ill of her and even my deceased baby brothers. It hurt deeply, and I couldn't fathom how people who were supposed to love us could be so cruel. The pain became unbearable, and I remember flee-ing my Grammy's house in tears, seeking solace from the hurtful words.

I never truly felt a genuine connection to my father's family. They treated me with kindness, but I always felt like an outsider. Meanwhile, my father, preoccupied with creating a new family amidst the chaos, would occasionally appear and make me feel like the luckiest little girl in the world. Every ounce of attention from him meant everything to me. I constantly searched for ways to make him want to be around me more, but no matter what I did, it never seemed enough. I was left yearning for his presence, his love.

As time went on, my father went on to achieve greatness. He remarried and started a beautiful family, seemingly doing every-thing right for them. He even embraced his new wife's children as his own. For years, I couldn't help but envy my siblings for simply existing. I believed that because I came first, I deserved at least a fraction of his attention. He was my father first. He used to call me Too-Dumsla (whatever that meant). He possessed an undeniable charm and wit, and his handsome, flashy demeanor captivated everyone around him. I, too, adored my father then, and I still do today. And now, I find solace in knowing that they were worth the changes he made.

F*CK AIDS!

As a young child, my world revolved around the moments I spent with my father's family, particularly at my aunt Rena's house. It was a place of pure joy and excitement, with its grandeur and constant buzz of activity. Surrounded by my cousins, laughter echoed through the halls, and there was always something fun happening. Unlike my grandmother's strict household, Aunt Rena's home was a haven of freedom. Every room boasted a television with cable, and the snack options seemed endless, igniting my youthful imagination. It was a place where I felt truly alive, where I could escape the confines of my own reality and immerse myself in the joyous chaos of family.

However, as I reached my mid-teens, my world was shaken to its core. It was then that my mother, with tears streaming down her face, confided in me, revealing the devastating news that her time on this earth may be limited. The weight of her words settled heavily on my young shoulders, and I struggled to comprehend the magnitude of what she was telling me. She urged me not to dwell on fear or worry, but instead, to make a difficult decision: who would I choose to stay with if she were to pass away? It was a decision no child should have to make, yet here I was, faced with the harsh reality of mortality.

My mother kept the details of her illness hidden from me, leaving me to wonder and speculate. I suspected it might be some form of cancer, but her reluctance to share the truth perplexed me deeply. Despite my confusion, I made it clear to her that if the need arose, I would find solace in the embrace of my beloved Aunt Rena. She had always been a pillar of strength and love in my life, and I knew that being surrounded by her warmth and the familiarity of my cousins would bring me comfort during such a difficult time.

Little did I know that the truth about my mother's condition, as well as my brothers', would remain concealed until I turned eighteen. It was during a routine visit to my OB- GYN, prompted by the discovery of a small lump in my right breast, that the shocking revelation unfolded. As the doctor delved into my medical history, he casually inquired about any family members who might have AIDS. Bewildered, I denied any knowledge of such a situation, adamantly stating that neither my mother nor anyone else in our family had AIDS. To my surprise, the doctor persisted, mentioning my mother by name and confirming that she indeed had AIDS. I was dumbfounded, unable to comprehend the gravity of the situation. Immediately after leaving the doctor's office, I dialed my mother's number, desperate for an explanation. The silence that followed on the other end of the line was deafening.

In that moment, I couldn't decide which emotion consumed me more: the shock of the revelation or the overwhelming sense of betrayal. How could my mother keep such a life-altering secret from me, her self-proclaimed best friend? It felt like a knife had been plunged into my heart, shattering the trust that had been the foundation of our relationship. As I sat in my car, the weight of the truth crushing down on me, I couldn't help but feel a sense of anger and confusion. I questioned why she had chosen to keep this hidden from me, denying me the opportunity to fully understand and support her through her battle with AIDS.

It was my first year of college, and my campus was an hour away from my mother's house. As I drove, my eyes fixated on the highway markers, each one passing by in a blur. My mother attempted to explain the situation, her voice filled with regret and remorse, but I felt numb, disconnected from reality. How could she have kept something of this magnitude hidden from me? If only I had known, I would have approached life differently, especially when it came to exploring my own sexuality.

As I arrived at my college campus, the weight of the truth still heavy on my shoulders, I knew that I had to find a way to navigate this new reality. The journey towards acceptance and understanding would not be easy, but I was determined to educate myself about AIDS and become an advocate for both my mother and myself. The secrecy and betrayal I initially felt slowly transformed into a fierce determination to fight the stigma surrounding HIV/AIDS and to ensure that no one else had to face the isolation and confusion that my family had experienced.

In the years that followed, I immersed myself in research, connecting with support groups, and educating myself about HIV/AIDS. I learned about the importance of early detection, the advancements in treatment options, and the power of empathy and understanding. Through this journey, I not only found solace and healing for myself, but I also discovered a deep passion for raising awareness and fighting for the rights and well-being of those living with HIV/AIDS.

While the pain of my mother's deception still lingers, I have come to understand that her decision to keep her diagnosis hidden from me came from a place of fear and a desire to protect me. In her eyes, she may have thought she was shielding me from the harsh realities of her illness, but in reality, she denied me the opportunity to fully support her and be a source of strength in her darkest moments.

Today, I carry the lessons learned from my mother's secrecy and my own journey towards acceptance. I am determined to break the silence and stigma surrounding HIV/AIDS, advocating for education, compassion, and support for those affected by this devastating disease. Through my own experiences, I have come to understand the power of honesty, open communication, and the importance of being there for one another in times of need. And while the wounds of the past may never fully heal, I find solace in the hope that my story can bring comfort and understanding to others who may find themselves in similar situations.

Let's take a step back.

ANOTHER NEW DAD?

As a child, growing up in a broken and unstable family, all I ever wanted was the warmth and stability of a normal family. But at the age of nine, my hopes were dashed when my mother remarried a man we'll call Slick. On the surface, Slick seemed like a kind and gentle person, always soft-spoken and charming around family and friends. However, there was something about his eyes that made me uneasy, a glint of something sinister lurking beneath his façade.

Behind closed doors, my mom and Slick would engage in constant arguments, their voices echoing through the walls and leaving me with a lingering sense of distrust. I vividly recall being in the backseat of my mom's car as she confronted woman after woman, accusing them of being involved with her husband. The memories are hazy, but I can swear we even barged into one woman's home, my mom's anger and pain fueling her relentless pursuit of the truth. Love and marriage, in my young mind, became synonymous with deception, infidelity, and abuse. I wanted no part in any of it.

Ironically, life had other plans for me, and I would come to experience these painful dynamics not once, but three times. Each time, it reinforced my belief that love was a treacherous path filled with betrayal and pain. One particular incident stands out in my memory, etched into my mind like a scar. We were temporarily staying at my aunt Grace's house, a luxurious mansion that seemed like a haven compared to the chaos of my own home. During those few months, I found myself alone with Slick one night while my mom was away. He asked me to perform some tricks for him, but insisted that I keep my pants off. I was around 11 or 12 years old at the time, and the discomfort I felt was overwhelming. It reminded me of another incident, a year prior, when a trusted family member violated my trust by touching me inappropriately while I slept. I initially thought it was a nightmare, but as I opened my eyes, I saw him clearly, indulging in his own perverse desires. I pretended to be asleep, waiting for him to leave the room before seeking refuge at my grandmother's house. I confided in her, and within half an hour, my mom arrived, embracing me tightly. I begged her not to confront the family member, fearing the fallout it would bring.

Returning to Slick, I never trusted him after the day I heard him brutally beat my mom. It happened after a birthday party she had thrown for him at our apartment. Their argument escalated, and my mom's voice grew louder and more desperate. Suddenly, her screams transformed into a gut-wrenching gurgle that still haunts me to this day. I rushed out of my room to witness a horrifying sight: blood splattered across the walls, my mom lying on the ground, battered and broken. The details of what followed are blurry, but I was told that I managed to contact my uncle, who then alerted the authorities. As they carried my mom away on a stretcher, her swollen lips and missing tooth stained with blood, I made a solemn vow to myself. I swore that I would never allow a man to lay a hand on me like that. Love, as I had come to know it, was tainted by toxicity, abuse, and infidelity. The only love I truly understood was the bond between my mom and me. Every other form of love, from my absent father to my estranged brothers, and now this monstrous stepfather, was filled with fear and uncertainty.

There was another terrifying incident that remains etched in my memory, a constant reminder of the horrors I endured. During one of their heated arguments, Slick locked my mom in the bathroom, trapping her in a claustrophobic space that mirrored the suffocating atmosphere of our lives. I was in my bedroom at the time, paralyzed by fear, unable to intervene or escape the nightmare unfolding before me. I could hear my mom's desperate pleas for me to call the police, her voice trembling with fear and desperation. But in order to reach the phone, I had to pass by Slick. He warned me, his eyes filled with malice, that if I dared to come close, he would strike me with a pair of pliers he held menacingly in his hand. The terror coursing through my veins made it impossible for me to move. I couldn't bear the thought of those pliers connecting with my head, the pain and brutality mirroring the chaos that had become my reality. I don't even remember if I managed to call the police or not; it's a memory I've tried desperately to bury deep within.

Love, for me, was synonymous with chaos, pain, and fear. I never wanted to be in a relationship or get married if it meant enduring such torment. But sadly, this was the only reality I knew. Toxic energy disguised itself as love, leaving me yearning for something more, something genuine and compassionate. I craved the warmth of a normal family, a love that didn't come with strings attached or bruises as souvenirs. My journey to find that love, to heal from the scars of my past, would be a long and arduous one. But deep within me, a tiny spark of hope flickered, reminding me that love wasn't meant to be this way, that there had to be something better waiting for me beyond the darkness.

CHAPTER

5

17 AND SHACKING

The school year of 1997/1998 was a tumultuous time for me. I found myself distanced from my mother, with whom I had spent most of my life. She made the difficult decision to allow me to live with my toxic boyfriend during my senior year in high school. It was a challenging situation, as she had relocated 50 minutes away and didn't want to disrupt my final year. Little did I know that this decision would introduce me to a world of infidelity and deceit, leaving an indelible mark on my young heart.

Spencer, my boyfriend at the time, possessed an undeniable charm and handsome appearance. He effortlessly won over my mother's affection, and she wholeheartedly approved of our relationship. In her eyes, he was the epitome of the kind of young man I should be dating. Spencer knew how to play the part, always behaving like a perfect gentleman whenever my mother was around. Little did I realize that his charm was merely a facade, concealing his true intentions. Once he had won my mother's trust, he began to manipulate and deceive me. Naively, I felt honored that he chose me over all the other beautiful girls in our school who admired him. We became inseparable, sharing every aspect of our lives. He even started attending church with me, further solidifying our bond.

However, our living situation was far from ideal. We resided with his mother, her girlfriend, his sister, and her boyfriend. His mother's mental health issues made for an unpredictable environment. One day, she would shower me with affection, and the next, she would harbor intense animosity towards me. I constantly felt unwanted and walked on eggshells, but my fiery spirit made it difficult for me to suppress my emotions. Spencer recognized my vulnerability and exploited it to his advantage. I desperately needed him and his family during this challenging time, and he shamelessly took advantage of my dependence.

Reflecting on those years, I am astounded that I managed to escape unscathed, both physically and emotionally. Spencer and I engaged in an intimate relationship akin to little jack rabbits, with little regard for protection. It is a miracle that I did not contract a disease or find myself facing an unplanned pregnancy. When Spencer's cousin, who harbored feelings for me, revealed his infidelity, I confronted him immediately. Although he never admitted his transgressions, his guilt was palpable. Cheating on me became his norm, and I, sadly, grew accustomed to being betrayed. After all, where could I go? But then, out of the blue, he dropped a bombshell on me: he wanted to take a break. He claimed that he saw a future with me as his wife, but he needed his college years to find himself. And just like that, he left me, leaving me shattered and questioning my worth.

My college years were brief, but they held a significant place in my heart. I enrolled at Monmouth University, a stone's throw away from the beach and not too far from my mother and church family. During this time, my faith played a pivotal role in my life. Church became my sanctuary, a place where I found solace and purpose. I immersed myself in various church activities, serving on the Praise & Worship team, choir, and even becoming a youth leader. My mother, a minister herself, exemplified a genuine and authentic faith that made the Christian walk alluring. Gospel music became the soundtrack of my life, as I sought to please God and navigate the challenges that lay ahead.

Throughout my journey, music has been my constant companion, a healing balm for my wounded soul. When life became overwhelming, scary, or filled with stress, I turned to music as a tool for restoration and solace.

Yet, amidst the trials and tribulations, it seemed as though my trauma was often dismissed or overlooked. The passing of my stepfather and brothers, the shocking revelation of my mother's AIDS diagnosis - all these significant events were met with a sense of indifference. I vividly remember the day I discovered my mother's condition. She was upset that the doctor had disclosed this information to me, but I couldn't help but feel hurt that she hadn't confided in me herself. To add insult to injury, her new husband had known before I did. I thought we were best friends, and the fact that everyone else was privy to this life-altering secret before me felt like a betrayal. In my initial shock and anger, I viewed her actions as selfish and unfair. It took time for me to understand that she was merely trying to protect me, but the initial revelation sent me spiraling into a whirlwind of emotions.

This was a season of betrayal, resilience, and the enduring power of faith. It was a chapter that shaped the woman I would become, teaching me the importance of trust, self-worth, and the healing power of music. Little did I know that this was just the beginning of a journey that would test my strength and resilience in ways I could never have imagined.

YOUNG FOOLS & OLD FOOLS

It was during that time that I crossed paths with a man, whom we'll call Tom. Tom was nine years older than me, making me a naive 19-year-old and him a mature 28-year-old. My experience with men and relationships was limited, leaving me vulnerable to manipulation. Our first encounter took place at my uncle's house, where I couldn't help but notice a flashy Infinity parked in the driveway. Feeling confident in my cute little crop top and red skirt inspired by Destiny's Child, I entered the house and saw Tom playing pool with my uncle. He stood tall at 6'4, with mesmerizing light brown eyes and long locs cascading down his back. As our eyes met, my uncle introduced us, and before leaving, Tom asked for my number. Little did I know, this encounter would shape my life in ways I couldn't have imagined.

At first, I couldn't fathom what a grown man like Tom saw in me, but I felt honored that he did. He presented himself as a gentleman, impressing not only me but also my family. He seemed intelligent, which only added to his appeal. Unbeknownst to me, I was about to embark on a journey that would challenge my innocence and lead me down a path of regret.

Our relationship took a drastic turn when I discovered I was pregnant. Inexperienced and unaware of the consequences, I had allowed this man to leave his mark on me. Perhaps I was numb to the situation or simply didn't care. Instead, I made foolish decisions that I would later come to regret deeply.

From the moment my mother discovered that I was expecting a child, her emotions were a complex blend of disappointment and excitement. It was an unexpected surprise that seemed to take us both on an emotional roller coaster. Despite her initial shock, a sense of joy quickly enveloped her. The mere thought of becoming a grandmother filled her with a sense of anticipation and exhilaration she hadn't experienced in a long time.

Her excitement was not unfounded. For years, she was given bleak predictions about her health. Doctors had grimly informed her that she wouldn't live long enough to witness some of the most significant milestones in my life. The prospect of seeing me graduate from high school, watching me exchange wedding vows, or meeting her grandchild, were all considered unlikely scenarios. Yet, here she was, defying all odds and looking forward to welcoming a new member into our family.

Early into my pregnancy, we started discussing the details of this new chapter in our lives. During one such conversation, she expressed a unique wish. She didn't want to be referred to as 'Grandma' by her grandchild. Instead, she chose the term 'Uma'. It was an unconventional choice, but it perfectly encapsulated her personality - distinctive, endearing, and full of life. She was eager to embrace this new role and the unique moniker that came with it.

When I finally mustered the courage to tell Tom about the pregnancy, everything changed. Before I even had the chance to inform him, I called my mother, who seemed to have already sensed the truth. Through my tears, I confirmed her suspicions, and Tom's reaction, though shocked, lacked any signs of disappointment. He assured me that he would be there for me and our child. However, around the same time, I discovered that Tom had been living with a woman, his long-term girlfriend, whom I had no knowledge of.

One night, driven by a mix of anger and hurt, I found myself standing outside her home, where Tom's car was parked. I couldn't contain my emotions and banged on the door, demanding answers. To my dismay, Tom emerged and humiliated me in front of her. He denied our relationship, labeling me as crazy and young, insisting that I leave. The pain of his rejection, witnessed by everyone present, was unbearable. I can't recall how my mother arrived at the scene, whether she had followed me or Tom had informed her, but I remember her picking me up from the middle of the street. Collapsed in tears, I was consumed by the hurt and disbelief that this man, who had taken advantage of me, could so easily dismiss me in front of everyone. My mother, in her infinite wisdom, managed to convince me to leave.

Eventually, my family confronted Tom, urging him to make a decision. To my surprise, he chose to end his relationship with the woman he had been living with. He expressed his desire to marry me and make things right. Deep down, I knew this wasn't what I truly wanted, but considering the circumstances of my pregnancy, it seemed like the best option. After all, he had chosen me over her. What right did I have to complain? Little did I know, this decision would prove to be one of the most foolish choices I would ever make.

I will never forget the moment we shared the news of my pregnancy with my grandmother. The shock and disbelief that washed over her face were palpable. I could almost detect a faint chuckle escaping her lips. No one, not even my own grandmother, believed that I, Esha, would be the one to carry a child. At that time, I was so consumed with my own self-image and body that the mere thought of becoming a mother seemed inconceivable. I had always maintained that if I ever did have children, I would adopt.

Perhaps it was the painful experiences of pregnancy and childbirth that I had witnessed my own mother endure, only to result in heartbreak and loss, that made me shy away from the idea of motherhood. I was determined to shield myself from that potential pain, so I firmly declared that I would not have children. But as life would have it, I was proven wrong once again.

The moment Khyturah entered this world, my entire existence transformed. From the very instant I laid eyes on her, I knew that I had to do everything within my power to provide her with everything I never had. Everything I had ever yearned for. She was the epitome of beauty, perfection personified. However, Khyturah was born prematurely, seven weeks ahead of schedule, which meant she had to remain in the hospital. Leaving her behind was the most excruciatingly difficult thing I had ever done. Two agonizing weeks later, I finally brought my precious baby girl home.

Eventually, Tom and I decided to get married at my church. Little did I know that this marriage would turn out to be a sham.

From the very beginning, Tom had managed to deceive me, presenting himself as a hardworking individual. But reality proved otherwise. Tom wouldn't lift a finger to work, even if his life depended on it. Don't get me wrong, he had a decent job when we first met, working at a hospital. However, he had a knack for losing and failing to maintain his positions. He was incredibly lazy, preferring to indulge in his own desires rather than putting in the effort to earn a living. Whenever he received his paycheck, he would splurge on personal items, clothes, and jewelry, neglecting his responsibilities of paying rent and bills. I was left to shoulder that burden entirely on my own. To make matters worse, he was unfaithful.

Intimacy between Tom and me was a rarity. I can't quite explain how it happened, but one night, against all odds, we found ourselves being intimate, and that's when I knew, in that very moment, that I was pregnant with Egypt. In January 2005, my baby girl Egypt was born. Egypt, my little twin was my absolute heartbeat. Her presence helped bring light to a very dark marriage.

In my mind, the relationship I had with Tom was far from what one would consider a typical marriage. It lacked the essential elements of intimacy, companionship, and partnership that are expected in a husband and wife relationship. Instead, Tom was merely a presence in our lives, a mere spectator, without actively contributing or participating in our household.

Financially, I carried the burden of paying every bill, shouldering the responsibility of our household on my own. This added strain on top of the lack of emotional connection made me far from happy, and I could sense that Tom was also unhappy in our marriage. His actions and words often made me question not only his love for me but also his true desires and intentions.

There were moments when Tom would hurt me with his harsh words, calling me ugly and suggesting that our daughters' beauty was solely attributed to him. These hurtful remarks deepened my doubts about our relationship and further diminished any remaining love or respect I had for him. It became clear that he was not the person who could love me the way I deserved to be loved.

Tragically, my mother's passing marked a turning point in my decision to leave Tom. Before she died, she had urged me to promise her that I would end my marriage to him. She had found true love in her life and believed that I, too, deserved to experience it. Her conviction and belief in my worthiness resonated deeply with me, and after her funeral, I made the firm decision to file for divorce.

During this tumultuous period, mourning my mother's death became an incredibly challenging task. The grief weighed heavily on me, and I found myself numb and unable to truly feel anything. It felt as though I was trapped in a state of stagnation while the world around me continued to move forward. My mother had been my guiding light, my rock, and my best friend. Losing her left me feeling lost and hollow inside.

Despite my own pain, I knew that I had to summon every ounce of strength within me for the sake of my daughters. They needed me to be strong, to be their support system in such a difficult time. So, I put on a brave face, pretending to be okay while struggling with my own grief.

In the end, it became clear that leaving Tom was the right decision. Not only was he absent during my time of grief, but he also added to my trauma by subjecting me to further emotional distress. The signs and confirmations I received after my mother's passing solidified my belief that I deserved better. I deserved love and happiness, and Tom was not capable of providing that for me.

So, after the funeral, I followed through with my decision and filed for divorce. It was a difficult and painful process, but it was necessary for my own well-being and the happiness of my daughters. I took the first step towards building a new life, one that would hopefully be filled with love, companionship, and the true partnership I had always longed for.

LOVE HURTS

I made a conscious decision to prioritize my career and my health after going through a difficult period in my life. I poured my energy into my professional success, working tirelessly to pursue my degree while also raising my precious daughters. I was focused and content, not actively seeking anything new or different.

But then, shortly after my mother passed away, I crossed paths with Jake. There was something about him that intrigued me, perhaps because he hailed from my hometown. I remember our first date in May 2007. Jake had a softball game that Sunday, and ordinarily, I would have been at church, singing and praising with my family. However, on that particular Sunday, I decided to skip and spend time with him instead. As I sat on the bleachers, cheering him on and reading my book, I couldn't help but feel a connection forming. After the game, when I suggested grabbing some food, he hesitated, claiming he wasn't very hungry. Deep down, I knew he wasn't being entirely truthful. Playing softball under the scorching sun for hours would surely work up an appetite. Eventually, he admitted that he didn't have the extra money for food, feeling a bit embarrassed about it. But for me, it was no big deal. I took him to Subway and told him to order whatever he wanted. From there, we went back to his apartment.

Jake and I connected on a level I hadn't experienced before. Like me, he had also lost his mother, although at a much younger age. He shared with me the hardships he had endured as a teenager due to this loss. I felt a deep empathy for him, and he reciprocated that empathy for me, as I had just lost my mother as well. It seemed as though he was the only person who truly understood the pain I was going through, so naturally, I gravitated towards him. In due course, I introduced Jake to my daughters. Khyturah was a bit hesitant at first, but she warmed up to him quickly. Egypt, who was just a toddler at the time, adored him. He had a natural way with my girls, and his presence brought a smile to my face.

When my ex-husband, Tom, discovered that I was dating Jake, he became incredibly upset. He pleaded and begged my family members to convince me to come back to him. However, the thought of returning to Tom never even crossed my mind. There was no love left between us, and being with him offered no benefits whatsoever. In my vulnerable state, all I craved was the love and understanding that Jake seemed to provide. Our relationship progressed rapidly, and within six months of dating, he proposed to me. I had no doubts in my mind that he was meant to be my husband. Up until that point, we had spent every single day together, and he had even moved in with me and my girls. It felt as though he worshipped the ground I walked on, constantly reminding me of my beauty and how fortunate he was to have me. Despite not earning much, he was always willing to give me everything he had.

However, everything changed after we got married. The day after saying our vows, I was introduced to a side of Jake I had never seen before - his violent left hook. It happened during our first disagreement, which arose after we were robbed of our wedding money by hotel staff. We found ourselves in the parking lot of a McDonald's in Bordentown when he suddenly struck me square in the face. That marked the beginning of almost a decade of physical and sexual abuse. When Jake first hit me, I turned to my uncles for support, expecting them to confront him or at least offer some form of protection. To my dismay, they dismissed it as a common occurrence in newlywed marriages, claiming that no marriage is perfect. With my mother no longer alive to guide me, I felt lost and numb, so I stayed. After all, where could I go? This was now my second marriage, and I had three children to consider. I felt fortunate that anyone still wanted me.

The most challenging aspect of being married to a monster is that no one outside our household knew the truth about him. To the world, he was charming, funny, and harmless. He had a knack for making people laugh and seemed incredibly patient. I could never understand why my family didn't see through his facade. Well, that's not entirely true. My grandmother, from day one, never trusted Jake. When she first met him, she noticed Egypt hugging his leg, and it didn't sit well with her. At the time, I couldn't comprehend her concerns, but eventually, I would come to understand them all too well.

Shortly after our wedding, I discovered that I was pregnant once again. Naimah, my beautiful surprise baby, arrived less than nine months later. I hadn't planned on having more children, especially without the support and guidance of my mother. I even expressed my doubts to Jake, fearing that I wouldn't be able to handle the emotional toll. However, having Naimah turned out to be the best decision I ever made. With her arrival, my circle felt complete - three incredible daughters who became my closest confidantes. That's why it broke my heart that they had to witness the physical and sexual abuse inflicted upon me by Jake. I thought I was hiding it from them, but they saw it all.

This chapter of my life, filled with pain and suffering, was marked by a silence that extended beyond the walls of our home. Nobody knew the torment I endured at the hands of my husband. He was a master at hiding his true nature, leaving me feeling isolated and trapped. I often wondered why my family didn't intervene, why they couldn't see the warning signs. Only my grandmother, with her intuition and wisdom, sensed something was amiss from the very beginning. Yet, I remained blind to it all, hoping for a better future for myself and my daughters.

I love my daughters.

In the depths of our time living in California, in a modest two-bedroom condo graciously leased to us by a kind-hearted woman, a haunting incident unfolded. It was a night when Jake, consumed by his furious rage, faced my confrontation about yet another affair I had just discovered. Infidelity had become his twisted norm, despite his promise to change when we left New Jersey. Here we were, on the other side of the country, and he had still managed to betray me. As I summoned the courage to confront him, I was met with a painful slap across my face. But that was just the beginning.

Jake's anger spiraled out of control, as he relentlessly pursued me through our home, hurling insults and venomous words in front of our innocent daughters. Dinner had just been lovingly prepared - a homemade feast of spaghetti and meatballs - only to be callously thrown over my head by the man who was supposed to love and protect me. In a desperate attempt to shield our girls from this horrifying scene, I urged them to seek refuge in their rooms. Fear gripped their little hearts as they witnessed the chaos unfolding before them. Unrelenting, Jake then turned to the refrigerator, pouring milk and anything else he could find over me. I rushed to the bathroom, desperately trying to cleanse myself from the burning tomato sauce that stung my eyes. But as soon as I wiped my face, he spat on me. In that moment, I felt utterly shattered, my self-worth crumbling to its lowest point.

This was just one of the countless episodes my precious daughters had been forced to witness. Recently, they reminded me of an incident that occurred when Naimah was only one year old. We were living in Ewing, New Jersey, and once again, Jake unleashed his fury upon me for daring to confront him about his latest transgression. He beat me mercilessly, leaving me battered and bruised, before stripping me of my dignity and leaving me abandoned in the street. My purse and keys were cruelly discarded on the roof of our house, while he heartlessly stole my car. All the while, my daughters stood helplessly at the front door, their innocent eyes absorbing the horrors unfolding before them. It was only through the kindness of teenage boys passing by that I was able to find solace, as they helped me to my feet and retrieved my purse from its lofty perch.

The abuse inflicted upon me by Jake was not confined to the walls of our home; it followed us wherever his temper flared. He attempted to push me out of moving cars, subjected me to public humiliation by stripping me naked in a New Orleans hotel room and locking me outside, and even dragged me down stairs by my hair, tearing it from my scalp. There was a time, when I was seven months pregnant with Naimah, that his rage led him to drag me down the unforgiving steps and lock me outside, leaving me vulnerable and terrified.

Mentally and emotionally, I was broken. How could this man claim to love me, yet continuously cheat on me and inflict such pain? I was lost in a bewildering maze of confusion, for when Jake's anger subsided, he could be charming, funny, and affectionate. It was this duality that made it agonizingly difficult for me to break free. No matter how deeply he wounded me, he always managed to find his way back into my heart.

As the trauma of our marriage continued to weigh heavily upon me, my desire for intimacy with Jake waned. In response, he callously took what he wanted from me, even when I was asleep. There were mornings when I awoke sore and bloodied, unaware of what had transpired during the night. It was only when I mustered the courage to feign sleep one night that I shattered my own heart. I was left disgusted by the realization that the man I once called my husband had taken advantage of me in the most despicable way. During those dark times, I sought solace in alcohol and marijuana, desperately trying to numb the pain. Sleep only came when I drowned my sorrows, but even then, Jake shamelessly exploited my vulnerability.

Though still bound by the chains of marriage, I had long given up hope on our union. What had being a "good wife" ever brought me, except heartbreak and anguish? I shouldered the burden of being the primary breadwinner, tirelessly caring for Jake, our children, and the household, all while juggling two jobs. My days were consumed by shuttling our girls to three different schools, driving Jake to his workplace forty minutes away, and then rushing to my own job. It was a never-ending cycle of devotion to Jake and our daughters. In the process, I had lost sight of myself. But amidst the darkness, music became my saving grace.

CHAPTER 8

SA'MONE SINGZ

In 2015, I made a life-changing decision. I realized that I could no longer be a victim to Jake's abusive behavior. The fear and constant anxiety had taken its toll on me, and I knew it was time to fight back. I mustered up the courage to ask Jake to leave, but to my surprise, he refused. He didn't want a divorce and believed that I would never leave him. In the past, his persuasive words had kept me by his side, and I had genuinely loved him. However, love alone was not enough to sustain me anymore. The final straw came when I discovered that he was pursuing the mother of his children. It was a painful realization that shattered any remaining commitment I had to him. I made it clear to Jake that if he chose to stay, I would no longer be faithful to him. Despite my ultimatum, he decided to stay.

During this tumultuous time, music became my refuge. I had always possessed a decent voice and a passion for songwriting. From a young age, I had formed music groups with my cousins and had always felt a deep connection to music, even during my church years. In 1998, I had the incredible opportunity to be part of a teenage ensemble called PRAISE, and we won the McDonald's Gospelfest, performing at Madison Square Garden. It was then that I realized music had to be an integral part of my life. Singing and writing songs allowed me to feel a sense of freedom and release.

Becoming an R&B artist elevated my passion for singing and performing to new heights. I channeled all the pain and hurt I had experienced into my music. Living in North Carolina at the time, I started performing at local events and clubs, slowly building my reputation. Eventually, I released an independent album titled "Good Girl Gone," pouring out my pain through my lyrics. However, I now realize that I was inadvertently inflicting my pain onto others through my music. I hadn't taken the time to process and heal from my own wounds. And then, the music industry showed its savage side.

The music industry can be a ruthless place, where only the strong or weak survive. I believed I could handle it, but the sudden attention was overwhelming. I transformed from the regular "Iesha" to "Sa'Mone," embracing the middle name given to me by my late mother. I had despised my middle name as a child, but after her passing, it became a source of love and connection. So, I became Sa'Mone, the "sexy red-head." I would wear long red weaves and provocative outfits during my performances. I gained recognition from my peers in the industry and even developed a genuine fan base.

Winning the Carolina Music Award for Best R&B Artist was an incredible moment in my career. It was a validation of all the hard work and dedication I had put into my music. As I stood on that stage, accepting the award, I felt a surge of emotions. I was on top of the world, proud of my accomplishments, and grateful for the recognition. It was a humbling experience that reminded me of the power of music and the impact it can have on people's lives.

However, amidst the excitement and celebration, there was a dark cloud hanging over my personal life. I had been unfaithful to Jake, my partner at the time, and it was something he was well aware of. Instead of feeling remorseful or guilty, I almost wore my infidelity as a badge of honor. I created songs and music videos that highlighted my indiscretions, almost taunting him with my actions. In my mind, I believed that he had never truly cared about me, so I didn't care if my actions hurt him. It was a selfish and destructive mindset that I now realize was fueled by my own pain and insecurities.

During this time, I found solace and companionship in one of my band members, whom I'll refer to as Smooth. Smooth was not only a talented musician but also someone who made me laugh and brought joy into my life. We connected on a deep level, sharing moments of genuine transparency and encouragement. We both had a deep connection with God, and it felt like we were spiritually aligned. However, looking back, I understand that what we had was driven by lust rather than genuine love.

Smooth became a pillar of support during my transition away from Jake. He was one of the few people who recognized that I was a victim of domestic abuse and urged me to leave. He wiped away my tears and provided the motivation I needed to overcome my pain. In the midst of our friendship, we fell into what we believed was love. I was deeply infatuated with Smooth, feeling like he was the one who truly understood and cared for me.

However, my world came crashing down when I discovered that Smooth's wife had no knowledge of his infidelity and had no intention of leaving him. A mutual friend revealed that they had recently shared an intimate event together, and it devastated me. I sat there, wearing a smile on my face, but inside, I was crumbling. The person I thought I could trust had lied to me and continued to be intimate with his wife. He claimed that he wasn't even attracted to her, which only added to my confusion and pain. In my darkest moments, I found myself resenting this woman for fighting for her marriage, feeling like she was standing in the way of what I desired.

Despite the betrayal, Smooth continued to oscillate between his wife and me. I allowed him to string me along, hoping that he would eventually choose me over her. It was a toxic and destructive situation that I couldn't seem to escape from. One night, when I couldn't get in touch with Smooth, my intuition told me that he was with his wife. Fueled by anger and frustration, I drove past his house and saw her car parked outside. It wasn't the first time I had shown up unannounced, desperately seeking answers, but it would be the last. We argued, and in a moment of uncontrollable rage, I lashed out and punched him in the face. It was an action that I deeply regret and one that I carry with me as a reminder of the damage I allowed myself to inflict.

For a long time, I believed that I was the victim in this situation. I dwelled in my pain and anger, blaming Smooth's wife for my own heartbreak. But as time passed and I gained clarity, I realized that I was not the victim. I had hurt that woman, someone who was innocent in this whole affair. My selfishness and disregard for her feelings had caused her pain, and that is something I will always carry with me as a heavy burden.

Looking back on these events, I have come to understand the destructive nature of my actions. I allowed my pain and insecurities to cloud my judgment, leading me down a destructive path. I hurt those around me, including someone who was undeserving of my anger and resentment. It is a lesson that I have learned the hard way, and one that has shaped me into a more empathetic and compassionate person. I have made peace with my mistakes, but I will always carry the weight of hurting someone else as a reminder of the consequences of my actions.

ALMOST DOESN'T COUNT

Meeting Mark at that show was an unexpected delight. Even though our encounter was brief, his presence left a lasting impression on me. Unfortunately, as time passed, the memory of our meeting gradually faded into the background of my mind. It wasn't until Mark reached out to me on Facebook that I was reminded of that special moment. His simple act of reconnecting reignited something within me, forever altering the course of my life.

From the very first moment we started communicating again, I was captivated by Mark's charisma. This caught me off guard, as I had recently decided to take some time for myself to heal from the wounds of my unsuccessful marriage. Despite my initial intentions, I found myself irresistibly falling in love with him at a surprisingly fast pace.

At the time, we lived in different states. Mark had recently relocated from North Carolina to Georgia. Despite the distance, he would make the effort to travel back to North Carolina just to spend time with me. There was something indescribable about Mark that set him apart from any other man I had ever known. His intelligence and self- assured demeanor were like a magnet to me. And his dark skin, beautiful eye lashes, and mesmerizing smile only added to his irresistible charm. Both of us were hesitant to rush into a committed relationship due to our past traumatic experiences. However, despite our reservations, our connection blossomed into a passionate love affair.

When Mark entered my life, my daughters had grown tired of the concept of "dad" and "stepdad". Their previous experiences with father figures had left them disappointed, so they weren't particularly thrilled about the idea of someone new coming into our lives. However, they could see the happiness Mark brought to me, and that was enough for them to accept him. They lovingly referred to him as "Mr.," a nickname that still brings a smile to my face to this day.

I met Mark during a particularly challenging period in my life. I had reached a point where I felt like I couldn't trust anyone, and that I was destined to be a perpetual victim. But something about Mark made me feel safe, as if I could finally open up about the traumas that had haunted me for years.

One evening, we sat down together, and I poured my heart out to him. I shared the painful details of the abuse I had endured, the feelings of abandonment that had plagued me, and the scars left by rape and molestation. It was an incredibly difficult conversation, but Mark listened attentively, his eyes filled with compassion. He didn't shy away from my pain, but instead, he helped me see things from a different perspective.

Mark gently reminded me that I wasn't defined by the terrible things that had happened to me. I was not a victim, but a survivor. He made it clear that he saw strength and resilience in me. His words acted as a soothing balm for my wounded soul, gradually shifting my mindset from one of self-pity to one of empowerment.

The more time I spent with Mark, the more I realized that I had built walls around myself to protect against further hurt. I had become loud and aggressive, projecting an image of toughness to shield myself from vulnerability. But Mark saw past that facade. He saw the pain and vulnerability within me, and he encouraged me to embrace it.

It was by no means an easy journey. I had buried my past traumas deep within me, never truly allowing myself to heal. But Mark was there every step of the way, guiding me towards self-discovery and emotional growth. He patiently helped me confront the pain I had long ignored, encouraging me to face it head-on instead of continuing to bury it.

However, it wasn't just my past that I had to confront. Mark had his own personal issues to deal with, and some of his decisions caused me immense pain. The hurt I felt slowly turned into a simmering rage that began to consume me. It was as if all the years of pain I had carried were now amplified by the new hurts inflicted by someone I loved.

In the sweltering heat of August 2020, my world came crashing down. Mark, the person I loved and trusted, dropped a bombshell and decided to end our relationship. I was left in a state of shock and disbelief. It was as if the ground beneath me had vanished, leaving me floating in a sea of confusion.

Mark had always seemed happy with me, and I had poured my heart and soul into our relationship. I believed that I had done everything possible to demonstrate my love and support for him. I had been there for him through thick and thin, nurturing his dreams and providing comfort during his moments of pain. Yet, despite my best efforts, he chose to walk away, just like others had done in the past.

The pain of rejection hit me like a tidal wave, overwhelming and unbearable. It stirred up old wounds of abandonment and made me question my own worth. I couldn't help but wonder if I was doomed to a life of loneliness and never finding true love.

However, even in the depths of heartbreak, I recognized that Mark had taught me invaluable lessons. Through him, I discovered my own capacity for healing and embracing my vulnerabilities. Though the pain of our separation was immense, I also saw it as an opportunity to continue my journey of self-discovery and personal growth.

With a heavy heart, I began the process of picking up the shattered pieces of my life and rediscovering my own strength. Seeking therapy became a crucial step in helping me navigate the resurfaced pain and trauma. I leaned on the unwavering support of my daughters and family, slowly but surely rebuilding my fractured confidence.

The road to healing was long and arduous, but I refused to let my past define me. I was determined to emerge from this experience stronger and more resilient, with a renewed sense of self-worth. As I pressed forward on this transformative journey, I clung to the lessons Mark had inadvertently taught me, grateful for the growth and self-empowerment that had blossomed within me.

Little did I know, the true reasons behind Mark's decision to leave would soon come to light, offering a deeper understanding of our breakup.

ROCK BOTTOM

August 19-20, 2020 will forever be the darkest days of my life. In the midst of my despair, I found myself in Georgia, struggling to find solace while raising my three precious daughters. The weight of depression consumed me, turning me into a mere shell of the vibrant person I once was. I cried ceaselessly, my tears blending seamlessly with the demands of my work. Music, once a source of joy, became a painful reminder of the anguish that enveloped me. The toll on my body was evident, as I shed over 30 pounds, with each passing day leaving me smaller and weaker. Sleep eluded me, and the only respite I found was in the numbing embrace of alcohol and marijuana. Pain became my constant companion, an unwelcome presence that refused to relent.

But it wasn't just the breakup with Mark that plunged me into this abyss. It was merely another cruel reminder of the unforgiving nature of the world. I couldn't help but question why my life seemed to be a never-ending cycle of pain. Why did those who professed their love for me always end up hurting me or leaving me behind? The loss of my mother, a wound that still bled fresh, and the stroke that left my father unable to be the father he longed to be, further compounded my anguish. It felt as though life, as though God, was playing a cruel joke on me.

Separated from my family in New Jersey, I was drowning in my despair. It was my cousin Tosha who sensed the depths of my depression and made the arduous journey to Georgia to offer me solace and support. My daughters, witnessing my mental and physical deterioration, reached out to her out of fear for my well-being.

In those moments, I truly believed that my existence was a burden to those around me. I convinced myself that the world, including my own daughters, would be better off without me. I felt like a malignant force, destroying everything in my path, and the exhaustion was overwhelming.

Amidst this darkness, there was a glimmer of hope. A high school friend, though weary from hearing about my pain, still attempted to check on me. I tried to reach out for help, but my cries seemed to fall on deaf ears. My daughters, bless their hearts, heard me, but they were just as lost as I was, unsure of how to alleviate my suffering. It was unfair to subject them to such weakness and brokenness.

Realizing that I was teetering on the edge of a precipice, I knew I had to make a change, and quickly. It took a harrowing incident, with firetrucks and police cars descending upon our grand mansion in Jones Creek, Georgia, to jolt me awake. The officers and counselors who arrived that day could have easily whisked me away to a hospital, but instead, they showed me compassion. In that moment, as I gazed into the tear-streaked faces of my three beautiful daughters, a flicker of strength ignited within me.

I began to alter my routines and habits, desperate to shield myself from any triggers that threatened to unravel me further. Healing and processing my pain were distant aspirations, but I did come to accept them, along with the consequences they brought. Mark and I, despite our breakup, remained friends, bound by a deep care for one another. During our relationship, we had both agreed that we weren't ready for more children. With his two daughters, his focus on establishing himself in his career and finances, and my own dedication to my daughters and professional growth, the thought of adding another child to the mix seemed unfathomable.

The journey ahead was far from easy, but I was determined to find my way back to the light. For the sake of my daughters, for the sake of myself, I would forge a new path, one that would lead me towards healing and rediscovering the strength I had lost.

After our heartbreaking breakup, Mark and I found solace in each other's arms, seeking comfort and intimacy. Despite the pain, I couldn't bring myself to be with anyone else but him. I settled for the fragments of his love that he was willing to give me, hoping it would be enough. We grew closer as friends, or so I thought. Little did I know that it was all a facade, a cruel deception that would soon unravel.

In November 2020, Mark and I shared a moment of intimacy, unaware of the life-altering consequences that awaited us. Despite being on birth control, I discovered that I was carrying not just one, but two precious lives within me. The news struck me like a thunderbolt, leaving me in a state of shock and disbelief. At

40 years old, with my daughters almost grown, I couldn't fathom the idea of starting over as a mother. It felt like a secret I would carry to my grave.

Mark's reaction mirrored my own astonishment. He was speechless, clearly not anticipating this unexpected turn of events. After all, we had broken up, and neither of us had planned for this or even considered rekindling our relationship. To my utter dismay, I learned that Mark had another baby on the way, conceived with a woman 20 years younger than me. Unbeknownst to both of us, he had been engaging in unprotected intimacy with both of us simultaneously. The realization shattered me, as it dredged up painful memories of my own mother's story.

The weight of the situation bore down on me, leaving me feeling disgusted and wanting nothing to do with Mark. If I chose to carry these twins to term, I would inevitably have to navigate some form of coexistence with him. In my desperation, I turned to my daughters, sharing the news of my unexpected pregnancy and seeking their guidance. Determined to break the cycle of exclusion I had experienced as a child, I vowed to be transparent with them and value their opinions. Their unwavering support overwhelmed me with gratitude and relief. They reassured me that I wouldn't have to face this journey alone, promising to stand by my side and help me raise the twins.

In the midst of the turmoil, their empathy and love provided a glimmer of hope, reminding me that even in the darkest of times, family can be a source of strength and resilience.

I love my daughters.

As the initial shock of the situation began to fade, a wave of excitement washed over me. Despite the challenges ahead, I couldn't help but feel a sense of anticipation about the arrival of the twins. Being a single mom had become second nature to me, so I wasn't afraid to take on this new chapter alone. Mark and I eventually sat down to talk through the chaos that had consumed us, and I mustered the courage to ask him about his intentions.

I explained to him that my plan was to raise our boys on my own, with him having the freedom to participate as he wished. But to my surprise, he proposed something entirely different. He wanted us to be together again, to raise our family as a united front. He promised me, with unwavering conviction, that I would never have to face the challenges alone. He assured me that he would always be there for our boys and me. It was a promise that I desperately wanted to believe, but little did I know that it was just another lie.

What hurts the most is that I allowed myself to believe him. I couldn't fathom how all of this would work, especially considering the presence of another woman who was carrying his child. I was still healing from that painful situation, and the thought of introducing more chaos into my life seemed unbearable. This young woman, pregnant with her first child by a man much older than her, was infatuated with him. I simply couldn't afford to invite that level of turmoil into my already high-risk pregnancy. Yet, Mark insisted that he only wanted me and even spoke of marriage. He was there for me throughout the pregnancy, my partner in every sense of the word. We made plans together, dreamed of starting businesses, and even contemplated moving to a different state. At the time, I was working three full-time jobs from home, pouring most of my income into Mark's ventures and endeavors. Little did I know that he was betraying me all along.

I found myself seven months pregnant with twins, juggling three jobs, raising my three daughters, supporting my oldest through college, and navigating the storm of a toxic relationship. I had strayed so far from my true self, sacrificing my own well-being day in and day out without any respite. Exhaustion had become my constant companion, and my body was beginning to bear the brunt of it all. Then, in July of 2021, I was confronted by one of the many women Mark had been unfaithful with. This young lady revealed that she and Mark had been intimately involved throughout our entire relationship, even going so far as to use my car and stay in the apartment I had helped him secure. And if that wasn't enough, the mother of his other child reached out to me, informing me that Mark had been attempting to engage in sexual relations with her. She had already given birth to their child by then. It shattered my heart and sent me into premature labor.

I was admitted to the hospital for a week to halt the labor, only to be sent home on bed rest. I continued working all three jobs but from the confines of my couch. I was utterly miserable. I felt enormous, not just physically but emotionally as well. I no longer recognized the woman staring back at me in the mirror, and it seemed that Mark and my daughters felt the same way.

My daughters, bless their empathetic souls, witnessed everything I did behind the scenes to keep our household running. They saw the pain I endured, yet I always managed to find a smile for them, no matter how deeply I was hurting. I never mistreated my girls, always striving to be the best mother I could be. But looking back, I realize that I should have been a better version of myself for them.

I love my daughters.

On that fateful August morning, as I bid farewell to my girls and felt the tightening of my contractions, I knew that the arrival of my twin boys was imminent. Despite the urgency expressed by my doctor, there were still tasks that demanded my attention before I could make my way to the hospital. Hours later, Mark and I finally embarked on our journey to meet our precious sons.

After a grueling c-section and three long days, we returned home to our girls, now joined by their new brothers, Kairo and Kian. These two little miracles filled our hearts with joy, but there was something in their eyes that stirred a bittersweet familiarity within me. It was as if I was looking into the eyes of my twin brothers, who had tragically passed away when I was just a child. Kairo reminded me so much of Skinny Minny (Hakeem), while Kian bore a striking resemblance to Fat Boy (Raheem).

The girls were instantly smitten with their baby brothers, showering them with love and adoration. Even Khyturah, who was living far away in Arizona, made sure to connect with them through daily FaceTime calls. Egypt, my middle daughter, stepped up to the role of a second parent, always lending a helping hand in caring for the twins. Her support became invaluable, especially after Mark made the difficult decision to leave our family for the second time. It wasn't an easy choice, but given the toxicity that had permeated our relationship, it was a necessary one for the safety and well-being of us all.

During those tumultuous days, my emotions were in constant turmoil, and sleep became a distant memory. Mark tried to assist, but the toxicity between us had reached such a point that it was safer for him to keep his distance. He had done things that could have potentially landed me in jail, and for the sake of our children, it was best for him to stay away.

The aftermath of our separation plunged our household into a deep depression. Sleepless nights, the weight of work responsibilities, the chaos stemming from Mark's other child's mother, financial struggles, and the challenges of finding reliable childcare all seemed to converge upon me. And if that wasn't enough, the entire household was struck by the merciless grip of COVID-19. I found myself battling the virus while caring for my children, all while trying to hold onto my job. It was undoubtedly the darkest period of my life. Yet, amidst this darkness, Mark never even bothered to check in on the twins.

So there I was, once again, facing the trials and tribulations of life alone.

ARIZONA, A JOURNEY TO FREEDOM

It was time for yet another move, another chapter in my tumultuous journey. From the bustling streets of New Jersey to the sunny shores of California, then finding solace in the rolling hills of North Carolina, and finally ending up in the sweltering heat of Georgia. Each place had left its mark on me, but Georgia had changed me in ways that felt unbearable. The weight of my pain and the consequences it had on my children became too heavy to bear. I knew deep down that I had to escape, not just for myself, but for the sake of my children. Staying there would have been my downfall. So, I mustered the courage to uproot our lives once again and start fresh in the distant land of Arizona. It was a leap into the unknown, far away from everything and everyone I knew, but all that mattered to me were my children. Somehow, the pain of abandonment didn't sting as much from a distance.

However, I must admit that I prolonged my healing journey by clinging onto the emotional and physical ties that still bound me to Mark. Despite his inconsistency in supporting our twins and his infrequent visits, I couldn't help but love him and empathize with his struggles. I went out of my way to create opportunities for him to spend time with his sons, hoping that it would bring us closer together. And every time he did visit, we ended up being intimate, caught in the web of our complicated situation. It was a constant battle within myself, torn between my despise for the situation and the comfort I found in his presence. Little did I know, while I was unknowingly supporting Mark, he had reunited with his other son's mother and started a new life with her in Florida. When I finally confronted him, his response echoed the very reasons that pushed me to leave him in Georgia. It was a painful lesson for me to learn, a reminder that our relationship was not about being together; it was about being present and actively involved in our twins' lives. I had to come to terms with the fact that this was not his priority, and no matter how exhausted I felt, I had to shoulder this responsibility alone. And so, I summoned the strength within me to face this reality head-on.

Arizona, with its vast landscapes and open skies, became my sanctuary, my chance at rebirth. It was here that I had the opportunity to completely start over, to discover who I truly was beyond the chaos and heartbreak. For the first time in a long while, I was truly getting to know myself, reconnecting with the seven-year-old Iesha I had long abandoned. This rebirth transformed my perspective on everything. It challenged me in ways I never could have imagined and unlocked parts of my mind and body that I didn't even know existed.

It took 43 years of self-inflicted suffering for me to finally understand how to break free from the cycle of pain. I had to confront and process every experience, every trauma, every calamity, every chaos, and every ounce of pain that I had buried deep within me. I had spent so long holding onto that pain, unknowingly attracting similar negative energy into my life. But in order to truly heal, I had to acknowledge and face that pain head-on. Unprocessed pain only leads to more suffering.

Spencer, Tom, Jake, Smooth, and Mark were not the root of my problems. I was. I carried a pain within me that unknowingly attracted similar energies, and life simply
unfolded accordingly. It wasn't personal; it was a reflection of the energy I was putting out into the world.

In the depths of my memories, I can still feel the warmth of a bustling village of people who once surrounded me during my younger days. Whether it was the joyous family gatherings, the comforting embrace of my church community, or the somber moments of bidding farewell at funerals, I was immersed in a network of support and love. However, as the years went by, that village slowly faded away, leaving me with an overwhelming sense of loneliness.

Fear began to grip my heart, causing me to push people away, terrified of the inevitable departure that seemed to follow every connection I made. I couldn't bear another goodbye. So, I made a choice to distance myself from everyone, except for my precious children.

But the loneliness was suffocating. My soul ached for the warmth of community and the embrace of love. Yet, what had it brought me thus far? Who would want to be involved with someone burdened with so much baggage? After 43 years of life, two failed marriages, and the responsibility of raising five children, I found myself adrift in an ocean of isolation that I had allowed myself to drift into.

Thoughts of my aunts and uncles, who seemed to have forgotten about me, tormented my mind. I couldn't help but dwell on the people who had promised eternal love but had callously turned their backs on me. My children had no grandparents, aunts, uncles, or cousins to lean on. Only me, their mother.

The weight of providing for my children fell solely on my shoulders, as their fathers provided little to no support. I juggled four jobs simultaneously to make up for the lack, never seeking child support from them. Perhaps it was empathy or maybe even pride that held me back from taking that step. Instead, I chose to work harder, determined to ensure that my children never experienced any form of deprivation.

My oldest child, Khyturah, had witnessed my struggles firsthand. However, by the time she was seven, I had introduced her to a life beyond poverty, vowing that my other children would never have to face it.

When the twins were on the way, Jake and I had planned to hire a nanny so that I could continue working remotely and he could focus on his business. With his sudden departure, the need for a nanny became even more pressing. I needed help just to get some sleep. From 6 am to 7 pm, I toiled tirelessly, determined to meet every single bill on my own. This unyielding work ethic allowed me to provide a spacious home where all my children could thrive. It allowed me to surprise Khyturah with her first car when she earned her driver's license and another when she graduated college. That meant a lot to me specifically because it reminded me of when my mom took her last $500 and bought me my first car. A blue 1986 Chevy Nova.

My children are my entire world, and I would repeat this journey a million times if needed, just to ensure their happiness and well-being. There is no lack within our little universe. Who needs a village when I have created my own? Their love surrounds me, and mine surrounds them.

I love my children.

I am no longer burdened by the weight of my pain and the mistakes of my past. Instead, I see them as stepping stones that have led me to this moment of self-realization and growth. I have learned to forgive myself for the choices I made and the hurt I caused, understanding that I was simply doing the best I could with the knowledge and understanding I had at the time.

With this newfound clarity, I am committed to making better choices and creating a life that aligns with my true values and desires. I am no longer afraid to take risks or step outside of my comfort zone, for I know that it is through these experiences that I will continue to learn and grow.

I have also come to appreciate the importance of surrounding myself with positive influences and supportive individuals. I have let go of toxic relationships and embraced those who genuinely care about my well-being. I now understand that true love and friendship are not about control or manipulation, but rather about mutual respect, trust, and growth.

As I embark on this new chapter, I am excited about the possibilities that lie ahead. I am open to new experiences, new connections, and new opportunities. I am dedicated to living a life of authenticity, honesty, and compassion, not just towards others, but towards myself as well.

I am ready to write a new story, one that is filled with joy, fulfillment, and purpose. I am ready to let go of the pain and embrace the beauty and potential that life has to offer. The next chapter is not just a continuation of my past, but a chance to create something entirely different, something that reflects the person I have become and the person I aspire to be.

And so, with gratitude for the lessons learned and excitement for what lies ahead, I turn the page and begin this new chapter with hope, determination, and an unwavering belief in my own strength and resilience.

EPILOGUE

In the depths of pain and despair, one can discover the incredible power of resilience. In "Unbreakable: Calamity Meets Resilience," we embark on a transformative journey, where healing, self-discovery, and growth intertwine to create a tapestry of strength and inner peace.

This book is a testament to the human spirit, showcasing the courage and determination to overcome adversity. Through the pages, we witness the profound healing that takes place when trauma meets self-empowerment, when pain ignites the flames of transformation.

Within these chapters, you will find stories of love, forgiveness, and acceptance, reminding us that even the darkest moments can lead to incredible self-discovery. Each page is an invitation to embark on your own healing journey, to embrace the power of self-reflection and self-transformation.

"Unbreakable: Calamity Meets Resilience" is a guidebook to finding inner strength and self-fulfillment. It illuminates the path towards self-acceptance, self-love, and self-forgiveness, showing us that we have the power to heal ourselves from the wounds of the past.

Through emotional and spiritual healing, this book offers a roadmap for navigating the depths of trauma and pain, leading us towards a place of wholeness and healing. It teaches us the importance of self-compassion, self-awareness, and the unyielding power of resilience.

As you close the final chapter of "Unbreakable: Calamity Meets Resilience," may you find yourself empowered, inspired, and equipped with the tools to overcome any obstacle that comes your way. May you embrace your own unbreakable spirit and step into a future filled with growth, healing, and inner peace.

Iesha Jenkins, author of "Unbreakable: Calamity Meets Resilience" is a courageous and vulnerable woman who has embarked on a profound journey of healing. A divorced mother of 5, she's recognized the importance of acknowledging and processing her pain with utmost care and has chosen to share her personal experiences in order to offer hope and healing to others. While still in the midst of her own healing process, the author believes that by sharing her story, she can provide solace to those who may be going through similar struggles. Iesha's childhood memories, filled with both joy and pain, have shaped her into the person she is today, highlighting the power of family, resilience, and finding beauty in even the simplest moments. Her dedication to her beloved children reflects her unwavering love and commitment, and her hope is that this book serves as a guiding light for those seeking solace and healing, reminding readers that even in the darkest moments, there is always a glimmer of hope.

Iesha and her amazing children.